To:

From:

Date:

The Ten Commandments for Little Ones

By Allia Zobel Nolan
Illustrations by Janet Samuel

HARVEST HOUSE PUBLISHERS

EUGENE, OREGON

To God, whose continuous blessings never fail to astound me; my husband, Desmond, for his love, support, and patience; my nieces and nephews here and on the Emerald Isle; and for little ones and their families everywhere.

–Allia Zobel Nolan

For Alice, with love.

–Janet Samuel

The Ten Commandments for Little Ones

Text Copyright © 2009 by Allia Zobel Nolan
Artwork Copyright © 2009 by Janet Samuel

Published by Harvest House Publishers
Eugene, Oregon 97402
www.harvesthousepublishers.com

ISBN 978-0-7369-2545-7

Original illustrations by Janet Samuel

Design and production by Mary pat Design, Westport, Connecticut

Printed in China

09 10 11 12 13 14 15 /LP/ 10 9 8 7 6 5 4 3 2

For You, Little One

God loves us all very much, but He has a special place in His heart for you, His precious little one. I'm sure you want to show God that you love Him right back, and the best way to do that is to obey His rules.

God wrote these rules down on two stone tablets a long time ago. He gave them to a man named Moses to share with everyone. These ten rules are called the Ten Commandments.

What's more, because God is love, His Ten Commandments are based on love: loving God with all your heart, mind, and strength, and loving and taking care of others as you would love and take care of yourself.

I wrote this book to help you learn about the Ten Commandments and how to obey them. So read this book often, and remember to ask God to help you keep His rules.

For Parents, Teachers, Grandparents, and Friends

This book provides you with a helpful tool to teach your little ones about God's Ten Commandments. It was created with simple language, child-friendly illustrations, and Bible references, so that young children can learn these rules in a less complicated way.

What's more, to make it easy for your little ones to process what they've learned, I've included a "Dig Deeper" section at the back. Use this section to help children express their feelings about the Ten Commandments and open a dialogue with you about the lessons they have learned. Children can also use the glossary to look up highlighted words and learn even more.

My hope is that this book will bring you and your little ones closer to God and to each other.

Allia Zobel Nolan

Background

A long time ago, God's people lived as slaves in Egypt. They cried out to God to free them. God heard them and sent a man to help.

The man's name was Moses, and one day, as he was taking care of his sheep, he saw a bush that looked as though it was on fire. Then he heard a voice like no other. It was God.

"Moses," God said, "tell the king to let My people go."

Moses was afraid at first, but God gave him strength and a helper…Moses' brother, Aaron. Moses and Aaron went to talk to Pharaoh, the king of Egypt.

"Let God's people go free," Moses said. But the stubborn king didn't listen.

So God sent trouble to the land. He sent frogs and flies and hail and darkness. But the king still wouldn't listen. Then God sent more trouble, and again more trouble, until finally the king told Moses, "GO!"

Moses gathered the people and they left. But the mean king changed his mind. He sent his army to chase Moses and God's people to the edge of the sea. But God parted the sea so His people could walk to safety.

God's people were finally free! God told Moses to lead them through the desert into a new land. Then, one day, God called Moses up to a high mountain. When he got there, he saw a big cloud. God spoke to Moses from the cloud.

He said, "I am the Lord your God who brought you out of Egypt, so that you are not slaves anymore."

Then God wrote the Ten Commandments on two stone tablets with His very own finger and gave them to Moses. Moses brought them down to share with the people.

These are the same ten rules we obey today. They help us love God better, get along with each other, and do what is right.

In Bible times, some people believed that things—such as the sun, moon, or even a statue of a cow—were gods, but they were wrong.

There is only one true God. He loves you, and He wants you to love Him and to remember that there is no other like Him.

Rule 2: Worship God, not things.

A long time ago, people made **idols** of gold, silver, wood, and stone, and they called those handmade things "gods." Though those were false gods, the people still bowed down and worshipped them.

To **worship** something means to fill our minds, our hearts, and our time with it. The real God wants us to worship Him alone. He wants us to love Him above all, and He doesn't want anything else to take first place in our lives—not toys, computer games, TV, friends, movies, books, food, or movie stars. Can you think of anything else?

Rule 3: Never use the name of God in a bad or careless way.

God's name is so special that in Moses' days it was only used by a **high priest,** and even then only on one day a year.

You should keep God's name special too. Be careful when you say God's name. Use it to talk, pray, or sing songs to Him. But if something surprises you or causes you to become upset, never say, "Oh, God!" or "Oh my God!" And, if you should slip up and use God's name the wrong way, remember, we all make mistakes. Talk to God about it. He'll hear you and forgive you.

Rule 4: Keep one day a week for God and rest.

The Bible says God made the world in six days. But on the seventh day He rested. God wants you to follow His lead.

While it's good to pray to God every day, God also wants you to set aside one day at the end of the week to spend quiet time with Him in worship. Because God created you, He wants what is best for you. He designed you for work *and* for rest and relaxation.

Rule 5: Be good to your parents, obey them, and show them your love.

Even before God gave Moses the ten rules, people were expected to **honor** their parents. God wanted to make sure people would always do this, so He made "honor your father and mother" the fifth rule.

God gave the work of looking after you to your parents. You can help your parents do a good job, and at the same time show God you love Him, by listening to them, doing what they tell you, and being as good to them as God is to you.

Rule 6: Do not let your feelings make you take a human life.

In the Bible story of Cain and Abel, Cain became so angry that he sinned by hitting his brother and killing him. He was **jealous** because he thought God liked his brother better. God doesn't want you to allow angry or jealous feelings to cause you to sin. Sin is a word for "doing something against God's rules."

Hating, or having bad feelings about someone, is the first step toward wanting to hurt or get back at them. God wants you to forgive others. That may be hard, but remember that God forgives you when you do something wrong. You should do the same with others.

Rule 7: Do not break your marriage vows—be faithful to your husband or wife.

When a man and a woman get married, they promise to only love each other, and not to love anyone else in that same special way.

Joseph worked for a married man. The man's wife wanted to love Joseph the way she loved her husband, but Joseph said, "No!" and ran away.

You should run away from people who want you to break your promises to God and to others.

Rule 8: Do not steal.

God helped a great leader named Joshua win a battle, but God told Joshua and his army not to take anything away with them afterward. However, when no one was looking, a man named Achan stole gold and clothes. God sees everything. He punished Achan for disobeying Him.

God doesn't want you to take anything that doesn't belong to you. That also means that if you cheat at school or while playing, you are "stealing" the win.

In God's eyes, you didn't win. You lost. God wants you to win **fair and square** and to get things the right way.

Rule 9: Do not lie.

In Bible times, fathers would give their **blessing** to their first-born. A man named Jacob lied to his father so he could get the blessing instead. Because he did this, he hurt God, his brother, and everyone in his family.

God doesn't want you to tell lies to get something or to get out of doing something. He wants you to tell the truth about yourself and your friends.

Rule 10: Don't covet, or long for what belongs to others.

The serpent told Eve she could be as smart as God if she ate a piece of fruit from one special tree. Eve wanted what belonged only to God, so she took the fruit.

God doesn't want you to wish for what someone else has—a toy, a video game, clothes, good grades, or a special friend. That's called "coveting," and it can lead you to break more of God's rules.

God wants you to be happy with what He has given you. Thank God for the good things you do have.

Digging Deeper

Now that you've read about the Ten Commandments, let's see how much you've learned. Look for the answers on the next page.

Questions:

1. Who did God give the Ten Commandments to?

2. The Ten Commandments are all about two things. What are they?

3. Who does God want us to worship? How many true gods are there?

4. Is it okay to say "Oh my God" just for fun or if you are not calling out to God, praying, singing, or worshipping God?

5. If you take a toy that isn't yours, what Commandment are you breaking?

6. Husbands and wives don't have to keep their marriage vows. True or false?

7. If you cheated on a test, is that the same as stealing?

8. Do you have to obey your parents even if you don't feel like it?

9. When you grow up, you still have to follow God's rules. True or false?

10. You may never kill another human, but what else doesn't God want you to do? (Look back at the sixth Commandment.)

Answers:

1. God gave the Ten Commandments to Moses.

2. The Commandments are all about two things: loving God and loving your neighbor. If you can remember these two things, it may help you remember all of the Ten Commandments. Here's why: If you love God with all your heart, you will worship Him, never use His name in a bad or careless way, and keep one day a week special for God and for rest. If you love your neighbor, you will be good to your parents, never take a human life, keep your vows, and you will not steal, lie, or covet what someone else has.

3. God wants us to worship Him and Him alone. There is only one, true God.

4. No. It is not okay to use God's name carelessly.

5. The eighth Commandment. It tells us that stealing is not okay.

6. False. Husbands and wives must keep their marriage vows.

7. Yes. If you cheat on a test, it's the same as stealing.

8. Yes. God wants you to honor and obey your parents.

9. True. No matter how old you are, you should obey God's rules.

10. You may never kill another person. But God doesn't want us to hate others, either. You can dislike what is bad and evil, including someone's behavior…how he or she acts, but God doesn't want us to hate people.

The Ten Commandments, the Bible, and You

Your Bible is a great place to learn more about the Ten Commandments. You can read the complete story in Exodus 19 and 20. You can also find other stories mentioned in this book in your Bible as well.

On page 12, read more about how God made the world in Genesis 1–3.

On page 16, read more about Cain and Abel in Genesis 4:1-16.

On page 18, read the story of Joseph in Genesis 37, 39–47, and 50.

On page 20, read more about Joshua and Achan in Joshua 7:19-22.

On page 22, read about Jacob and the blessing in Genesis 27.

On page 24, read more about Eve and the serpent in Genesis 3.

Note to Parents, Grandparents, Teachers, and Friends

Use the prompts below to help children talk or write about their feelings regarding the Ten Commandments.

I want to love God with all my heart. I can show Him that I do by...

I spend a lot of time playing games and watching TV. Maybe I should spend more time talking to God instead. I could tell Him about...

Here's a prayer I wrote to honor God's name...

One way to obey my parents is to...

When I get angry, I can ask God to...

I made a promise, but I didn't keep it. I don't want to do that again, so I'm going to...

I took something that wasn't mine. I felt okay for a while, but then I felt...

God has given me so many things. I thank Him for...

Words and Their Meanings

B

blessing—in Bible times, a father gave his firstborn son a blessing, which meant he wanted God to protect and provide for him. It also meant the father passed along land and made that son the head of the house.

F

fair and square—winning a game or a contest, or passing a test, or being the best at anything fairly, without cheating.

H

high priest—back in Bible times, there were men who gave their lives to serve in God's holy place.
honor—to treat as very, very special; to look up to.

I

idol—a false god. It can be an object, figure, statue, or image people make and then pray to and worship. You make an idol of something when you put it ahead of God.

J

jealous—when you have bad feelings because someone else has something you want, is better at doing something than you are, or may be more popular than you are.

L

long for—when you wish or want something so badly that you can't enjoy what you do have.

V

vow—a promise you make to God, a person, or yourself.

W

worship—to give all your love, praise, and thanksgiving to something, to make that something number one in your life. You should only worship God.

I will show kindness...
to those who love me and
keep my commandments.

Deuteronomy 5:9

HOW TO WRITE
LETTERS
AND
E-MAIL

CELIA WARREN

QEB Publishing

First published in the United States by
QEB Publishing, Inc.
23062 La Cadena Drive
Laguna Hills, CA 92653

www.qeb-publishing.com

Library of Congress Control Number: 2007000928

ISBN 978-1-59566-346-7

Written by Celia Warren
Designed by Jackie Palmer
Editor Louisa Somerville
Illustrations by Tim Loughead
Consultant Anne Faundez

Publisher Steve Evans
Creative Director Zeta Davies
Senior Editior Hannah Ray

Printed and bound in China

CONTENTS

ALL KINDS OF LETTERS

Ever since writing was invented, people have communicated through letters and other kinds of written messages. With the arrival of electronic mail (**e-mail**), we still spend much of our time sending each other written messages. Here are some examples of ways we communicate in writing.

Friendly letter

If you write to someone you know well, you can use a relaxed **tone**, as if you were talking to the other person. This is suitable for a catch-up letter to a friend or a thank-you letter to a relative.

*Always start a letter with a **greeting**, such as "dear."*

Dear Susy,
It was great to see you on Sunday...

...and I would love to meet up again soon.
Love,

*Use a **comma** after the person's name.*

Tip

Your **closing** should say "regards," "kind regards," or "best wishes" instead of "love," if it's someone you don't know that well.

Postcard

It's common to send postcards to good friends, family, and neighbors, so they are usually **informal**. There's a picture on the front of a postcard. Your message and the address of the **recipient** goes on the back. There's not much room to write. So keep the message brief and write small!

Having a fab time here in the mountains. Our hotel is just across a wooden bridge. It's really comfy but there's no TV. I don't really mind because there are plenty of things to do. Climbed to the top of Craggy Hill today and swam nearby. Food's great. Weather's fine. See you soon. Love, Carl.

On a postcard, save space by skipping the greeting.

To save space, don't use full sentences.

More formal friendly letter

When you write to someone you don't know well, you should use a more **formal** style.

Dear Mrs. Dusty,
I really enjoyed my visit
to the Museum of...

Sincerely,

The **closing** is separated from your **signature** by a comma.

Tip

In business letters, start with
• Dear Sir: (to a man)
• Dear Madam: (to a woman)
• Dear Sir or Madam: (if you don't know which, and can't find out)

Business letter

Sometimes you may need to write to someone whose name you don't know or choose not to use.

107 Darby Avenue
Smithtown, MD 23957

April 15, 2007

The Director
Stuffwells Taxidermists
19 Rose Drive
Smithtown, MD 23958

Your address comes first.

Put the name and address of the company above the greeting.

Tip

Put two line spaces between each section of a business letter.

People tend to start e-mails with "Hi," especially to friends and family.

E-mail

The fastest way to communicate in writing is by e-mail. You send a letter typed on your computer to the computer of the recipient. They can then open your e-mail and read your words on their screen. You can also send attachments (word files or pictures) with your e-mail for the reader to open and look at.

Subject: HOW R U?
From: Jade Jones <j.jones@urserver.com>
To: Susie Smith <s.smith@supersupplier.net>
Hi Susie,
Just deleting old mails and reread yours. Sorry I never replied—been so busy! How are things? Have you heard from Jack? I saw him last week at the rock festival. Took funny pic (see attached jpeg).
See ya!
Jade

Shortened words and incomplete sentences are fine in informal e-mails.

LAYING OUT LETTERS

There are different ways of laying out friendly letters compared to business letters.

Tip

Put a sheet of lined paper underneath your plain paper to keep your writing in straight lines. It looks better than writing on lined paper.

Friendly letter to a grandparent

The date goes on the right below the address.

Write your address in the top right-hand corner of the page.

22 Stables End
Charlotte, WV 32357

January 17, 2007

Dear Grandpa,

Thank you so much for the money you sent me for my birthday. I'm going to spend it on...

Love,
Jon

*If you have paper with a **letterhead**, you only need to put the date before starting your letter.*

The Spinney
25 Long Lane
Doghill, NY 22915

January 17, 2007

Dear...

Springboard

Use one of the following street names as inspiration for who you are, where you live, and what you are writing about. Create a name for yourself and for the person you are writing to. Make sure you lay out your letter in the appropriate **format**.

Highwire Street
Juggler's Lane
Custard Avenue
Small Street

Cottage Road
Jolly Roger Road
Point Place
Cornwall Circle

Business letter to a bank manager

Put your own address at the top left of the page.

12 Baker Street
Seacrest, NJ 10707

April 13, 2007

The Manager
Fairford Bank
1801 Whistle Street
Seacrest, NJ 10707

Write the recipient's address underneath the date.

Dear Madam:

I am writing in reference to the Young Saver's Account advertised in this week's *Fairford Gazette*. I am interested in learning more about the program. Please send me more information at the above address.

Thank you,

Molly Beer

Molly Beer

*SAE enclosed

Business letters look best typed, not written by hand.

Begin business letters with a formal greeting, such as "Dear Sir/Madam:" or "To Whom It May Concern:." Write the greeting on the left of the page, underneath the recipient's address. In the first sentence, explain why you are writing and how you got their details.

When you address an envelope, start halfway down the envelope and left of center. Begin each line of the address directly under the one above.

*SAE
SAE stands for "stamped addressed envelope." Including an envelope that is stamped and addressed to yourself encourages the recipient to reply to your letter at no cost to himself or herself. It's a polite thing to do if you have asked for a response.

Molly Beer
12 Baker Street
Seacrest, NJ 10707

Tip
Do not include a SAE in a friendly letter. If the recipient intends to reply, he or she will happily pay for postage because you are a friend. If you include an SAE to them they will probably be either offended, or feel pressured into writing—or both!

FINDING YOUR VOICE

When you write a letter, it is important to write clearly so that what you say will be understood. You don't have your voice or facial expressions to convey your message. As you write your letter, picture the person who will be reading it. Imagine how they will react to your words. From your opening line, you set the tone of your letter. Make sure you continue to the end in the same "voice" as you started.

Misunderstandings

When words are spoken face to face, the listener can see your eyes and the expression on your face to judge your intention. If you say something that they misunderstand, you can correct your words right away.

In a letter, the recipient can only judge what you are saying by the words you have written. They might misunderstand what you are saying. This is especially true in the case of jokes. Make sure you joke only to people who know you very well and understand your sense of humor. Otherwise they might not realize that you're joking and could be upset.

Tip

Reread your letter before mailing it to make sure everything is clear. You could even pretend to be the reader opening the letter to help you to understand his or her viewpoint.

If you are writing a business letter:

- Begin with "Dear Sir" or "Dear Mr. Smith" (or "Dear Madam"/"Dear Mrs Smith"). Use a colon after the greeting.
- Use phrases like "I would" and "Could you please."
- Do not use contractions, such as "I'm" and "won't."
- Don't use slang words, such as "fab."
- End your letter with "Thank you" or "Sincerely."

If you write a friendly letter:
- Use the person's name or nickname, such as "Dear Mo."
- It's fine to use contractions, such as "I've" and "shouldn't."
- Use adjectives like "cool" or "fantastic."
- End your letter with "Love."

A

I think it's a shame you won't be at my party. I really wanted you there. You will miss all the fun.

C

What a shame you can't make it to my party. I understand why you can't come, but I'll miss you. Let's get together next week and I can tell you all about it.

B

I am disappointed you can't make it to my party. It won't be the same without you there.

A. This sounds a little selfish. The first two sentences both start with "I." Your friend might think that you didn't understand that she really wanted to come to the party, but couldn't. This letter might make her feel guilty, which would be unfair because she was truly sad to have to miss it.

B. This sounds a little bit better than A. But the reader might think you are disappointed in her personally, rather than disappointed about not seeing her at the party.

C. This version sounds the best. It focuses on the reader, rather than the writer. It suggests sympathy and understanding, rather than blame. It also ends on a positive note, suggesting a fresh opportunity to meet.

Springboard

Pretend to be the hostess of a party. Try finishing letter option C. (Begin the letter with "Dear.")

THANK-YOU LETTERS

Thank-you letters can be very easy or really hard to write. A lot can depend on the following factors:

- What you are saying thank you for: perhaps a kind deed, a thoughtful present, or a party you attended.
- How well you know the generous person—very well, a little, or not at all.
- If you expected the present or help, or if it was a surprise.
- If you liked the present or party.
- If you are writing for yourself or on behalf of a group of people.

Being polite

What if Aunt Julie sent a present you hate? Maybe it's an ugly doll with purple hair, a set of baby bath toys, or a hideous sweater. How can you be polite about it?

Tip

Find something positive to say, however loosely linked to the gift. For example:

- What a surprise those bath toys were! Mom will expect me to take baths now!
- Thank you for the lovely sweater. It's my favourite color! It must have taken you years to knit.
- Many thanks for the doll. I had fun choosing a name and decided that Maxi suits her best.

ACTIVITY

Try writing a thank-you letter on behalf of your class to a theater group that recently visited your school. Things for you to think about include:

- What did they perform? What was special about their act?
- Did your class join in? If so, how?
- How did you and your friends react and respond?
- Would you like them to come again?

Dear Actors,

I am writing on behalf of Class... following your visit to our school last week...

Springboard

Write a thank-you letter for a strange gift whose purpose you can't figure out!

WORDS TO HELP YOU: fascinating, intriguing, interesting, unusual, fun

Thanking strangers

It might seem odd to write and say "thank you" for a gift from someone you don't know, but it can happen. Parents have many friends. Perhaps one of them met you when you were a baby and still sends you a present each year. You don't know the person, but you have to say "thank you." What can you write about?

Tell the reader the purpose of the letter.

Give reasons why she made an especially good choice. Phrasing the first reason as a question sounds friendly—as if you were talking to her.

Dear Great Aunt Julie,

I am writing to thank you for the lovely scarf you sent for my birthday. Did you know yellow is my favorite color? It's so warm! I wore it when I went ice-skating with my friends last week.

Mom tells me you used to go ice-skating with her when you were my age. I wonder if you fell over as often as I did? Probably not—who could beat my record?

Next week we go back to school. I'll be in a new class with a new teacher. Everyone who was in her class last year calls her The Dragon. I hope my scarf has protective powers to save me from dragons!

Hope you are doing well.

Best wishes,

Dale

PS Mom sends her love.

Shows you know who she is and suggests you are interested in her, not just her gift.

Offer something interesting for her to think about: a glimpse of what is happening in your life. The scarf gets another mention—not essential, but an added bonus!

Informal closing words are more friendly than "sincerely."

The letters **"PS"** stand for postscript (Latin for "after writing")—useful for adding afterthoughts, separating them from the letter's main purpose.

LETTER TO A PEN PAL

A pen pal is someone you write to who you've probably not met. They may live in another part of the country or even the other side of the world. Or perhaps your pen pal is someone you met on vacation and you decided to keep in touch. Keep in mind that English may not be your pen pal's first language. If that is the case, use simple words and phrases in your letters.

Tip

You don't want your letter to read like a page from a diary. Nor do you want it to read like an **autobiography**— "My Life So Far." Avoid beginning every sentence with "I" (though it's fine to use once in a while).

Why write?

You are writing to each other to be friends. You could share information about:

yourself, your home, your family, and any pets

your school and friends

your hobbies and the kinds of films or music you like

11 Bruton Street,
Wingford, CA 43567

June 11, 2007

Dear Carlos,

My name is Jake and I'm 11 years old. My sister Molly is two years older. She has a pet guinea pig, and I have two rats named Tricky and Nibbles. Sometimes they play together. Do you have any pets?

My best friend is named George. We both have video game consoles that we play together after school. Math is my favorite subject at school. It's cool! Tomorrow, we're going to see a new sci-fi film.

Hope to hear from you soon. Please tell me all about life in Spain!

Your new friend,

Jake

Add a friendly sign off!

You want to learn about your pen pal to see if you have things in common and will get along well.

12

ACTIVITY

Even before you find a pen pal, you can plan the first letter that you will send to them. Tell them all kinds of things about your town and local environment. Remember that things which seem ordinary to you, might be interesting for someone from somewhere else. What would you like to know about your future pen pal's town and life?

Tips on finding a pen pal

- If your school has links with a school in another state, they may be able to help you find a pen pal.

- If your hometown is a member of Sister Cities International, your school may belong to the Sister Schools Program. It has links with schools all over the world and can put you in touch with a pen pal.

- Write a letter to your favorite magazine asking if another reader would like to **correspond** with you. (The magazine should not publish your address, but will send you any **responses**.)

Signing off

You can't write "Love" when you don't know somebody very well. "Best wishes," "All the best," or "Regards," are all fine. You are opening doors to friendship without assuming you will be great pals right away. When you first write to a new pen pal, you will need to include your last name in your sign off. You don't need to include it in later letters.

Springboard

Imagine that another planet has recently made contact with Earth. Write a letter from an alien who lives on that planet. Tell your human reader all about yourself and your planet. You might even enclose a recent "school photo" of yourself!

LETTERS TO OFFICIALS

One reason that people write letters is to express an **opinion**, but why do people put their feelings into writing? And where do they send their letters?

TO MAKE SOMETHING HAPPEN

Reasons for writing

You may want to write an official letter for one or more of these reasons:

TO HIGHLIGHT A PROBLEM, SUCH AS A SAFETY ISSUE

TO PREVENT SOMETHING FROM HAPPENING

TO COMPLAIN

Sending it

When you write to express an opinion, you want someone to take notice and act upon what you have to say. That is why it's important to send your letter to the appropriate person. Don't complain to the city council about getting too much homework; they can't do anything about it! Don't write to your teacher to complain about the movie theater closing. It has nothing to do with her!

Tip

If you cannot find out whom to write to, perhaps the editor of the local paper will know. You could always write to the paper with your concern, in the hope that they might print your letter.

ACTIVITY

Imagine that the city council plans to change the local park into a golf course. With a group of friends, write a series of letters to the council and/or the editor of the local paper about the golf course proposal. Adopt the points of view of different members of the local community, such as:

- Local golfers. They think it's great—or most do. Some say they won't be able to afford the higher proposed membership fees.
- The local wildlife society. It is not happy. Its members say that rare insects and birds will suffer if the trees are cut down.

Remember that these will be business letters, so begin with "Dear Sir/Madam" and close with "Thank you."

PARK TO BECOME GOLF CLUB!

Plans were unveiled today by Jobsworth District Council to turn Greendale Park and Leisure Amenity into a state-of-the-art 18-hole golf course.

...residents were up in arms at the proposal of

Springboard

Write a letter to a celebrity asking them to visit your friend who has been in hospital for a long time. Explain why you chose them, how their visit will speed up your friend's recovery, and why your friend deserves a visit. This time, instead of "Dear Sir/Madam," use the celebrity's name. Close with "Sincerely."

23 Greendale View
Jobsworth, VA 23456

June 16, 2007

Jobsworth City Council
Jobsworth, VA 23456

Present the situation.

Dear Councillor Brown:

Express your opinion.

I am really worried about the plan to turn the local park into a private golf club. I am a ten year-old who plays there regularly and I don't want this to happen.

My brother and I have played there all our lives, as did my parents when they were children. We also take swimming lessons at the swimming pool in the park.

If the park and pool close, we will have nowhere safe to play. The nearest swimming pool is ten miles away. For our safety, we must learn to swim because there are rivers and a reservoir nearby.

Make a suggestion.

Golf players are mostly adults who can drive out of town to play golf. You should use wasteland as the site for the golf course, instead of the park.

Request some specific action— including a reply to your letter.

Please take my opinion seriously and talk about it at your next meeting. Please write and let me know what you're going to do.

Thank you,

Make sure your whole letter fits on one side of a sheet of paper.

15

DRAFTING A REPLY

Sometimes you will receive a letter that needs a reply. It is often best to **draft** your letter before you send it. Read this letter and think about how you might respond.

ACTIVITY

Draft a letter of response. Here are some things for you to think about as you draft your letter:

Dear Reader,

SPECIAL ADVENTURE VACATIONS

Are you between the ages of 7 and 13?

Do you like fun and adventure?

Have you ever wanted to learn new skills and test them to the limit?

Would you love to make new friends in an exciting environment?

If so, then you could enjoy a Special Adventure Vacation in a beautiful region of lakes and mountains with like-minded people your own age.

We are offering ONE FREE PLACE on this vacation of a lifetime. If you would like to be considered, write and tell us what strengths you would bring to the experience and what you would hope to gain from the trip. Also tell us which outdoor event you would most like to try and why: kayaking, caving, archery, white-water rafting, scuba diving, mountaineering, canoeing, or sailing.

Write to Harry Bold at:

Special Adventure Vacations
14 Becky Lane
Lake Oswego, NY 12156

I look forward to hearing from you.

Sincerely,

Jane Gray

PP Harry Bold

- Include a brief introduction: say who you are and how you received the letter of invitation.

- Include a **paragraph** about your outdoor activity experiences so far.

- Try to answer all Mr. Bold's questions.

- Think up good reasons to back up all your **statements**.

The letters "pp" stand for "per persona" (Latin for "for the person"). They are used when someone signs a letter on behalf of another person.

- Write your address and the recipient's address in the correct places.
- Write the date.
- Decide whether to write "Dear Mr. Bold," using his **title**, or "Dear Harry." What effect will each choice have?
- Start a new paragraph for each part of your letter.

Springboard

Draft a reply to one of these letters:
- A request from your favorite pop star asking you to join their band.
- A letter from your best friend who has moved to Australia.
- A letter from an alien inviting you to visit planet Zog.

22 Dog Lane
Block Island, RI 02137

June 7, 2007

Special Adventure Vacations
14 Becky Lane
Lake Oswego, NY 12156

Dear Mr. Bold:

I picked up a copy of your letter at a local park. I am writing to win a place on a Special Adventure Vacation this summer.

As an active ten year-old, I like many sports. Recently, I got my life-saving swimming certificate and would love to try scuba diving and canoeing.

I've always wanted to visit the Great Lakes, so I hope you will consider offering me a place. My teacher says I'd be good at kayaking, but I can't afford classes. This vacation would provide me with the perfect opportunity to learn.

I hope I have convinced you of my enthusiasm and look forward to hearing from you.

Sincerely,
Sam Smith

After you have written your draft, read it aloud.

- Are your sentences short and to the point? If you run out of breath reading a sentence, then it is too long. Break it up into shorter sentences.

- Does your letter fit on one side of the paper? If not, then find ways to shorten it. Make sure you haven't said the same thing in different ways.

- In your last paragraph, summarize the main points of the letter.

SENDING POSTCARDS

People often send postcards to friends and relations when they go on vacation. But you don't have to be on vacation to send a postcard. You might send one to a friend to show them the town or area where you live. Postcards are also a useful way of keeping in touch or sending a short message.

Unique message

What you write on the back of a postcard makes it more interesting and personal. There is not much space on a postcard, so it's often best to leave out a greeting. The name and address make it clear to whom you are writing.

Tip

When you send vacation postcards you can usually write more or less the same message on each one. However, if you are sending a postcard to two friends or relatives who will compare cards, remember to choose different pictures and think of new things to write on each card.

You could tell your friends about:
- a fascinating fact about the place where you are staying
- what you did yesterday
- what you hope to do tomorrow
- how you find the local people and their customs
- if you have had a chance to practice a foreign language
- what the food and hotel are like

As space is limited, you can skip a few words, such as "the" and "I"—the reader is smart enough to work those out for themselves!

Paragraphs can be ignored, too.

Staying in a great hotel! It's got everything: pool tables, jacuzzi, sauna, and pool! Tomorrow, going rock climbing–can't wait! They provide safety gear, so I'll see you back at school next semester, don't worry!
Bye for now,
Charlie

Mr. Simon Pomfrey
4545 Zoey Ave
Martin, NV 85467

ACTIVITY

Try designing your own postcards.
Here are some ways you can make them:

• Draw and color a picture on an index
card or a rectangle of white card
about 4in. x 6in. It can be a picture
of anything; your pet, a place that you
love, or your house. Cover it with clear
contact paper. On the other side of
the card draw a line down the middle,
a rectangle where the stamp goes, and
lines for the address.

• Design your postcards on a computer
and print them out. You could use
digital family photographs or photos
of scenery. You could divide the
postcard into quarters and put a
different photograph—or clip art—in
each section.

• Make a collage from things you have
collected from your vacation: cut-outs
from photos or brochures, tickets,
menus, pressed leaves, and flowers.
Stick them onto a rectangle of card
and cover with clear contact paper.

Tropical sunset, Bali

glue stick

Springboard

Buy or make a postcard to send
to someone who may not get
much mail. For example, a
grandparent who lives far away,
or a great aunt or uncle. You
could even send it to a neighbor
as a surprise!

19

SENDING E-MAIL

Letters don't reach their destinations until at least the next day, which is why they are sometimes called "snail mail." By contrast, you can type an e-mail in a few seconds, press send, and it's gone. Your recipient can read it almost immediately.

Replying to e-mail

To reply to an e-mail that you have received, click "Reply." Your **correspondent**'s e-mail address will appear in the To line. The Subject line will say "Re:" followed by the original subject. "Re" means "regarding"—so your reply will be, for example, "Re: Movie Trip." Then you can add your message, such as: "OK. Meet you by the popcorn stand."

ACTIVITY

Try adding a signature line to an e-mail. This could be your favorite catchphrase or quotation. In the "Tools" drop-down menu, go to "Options," then choose "Signatures" to create a signature. Click the signatures icon to add it to your e-mails.

Drafting

It is best to draft important messages first. Save an e-mail as a draft by going to "File" then clicking on "Save as Draft," rather than sending it right away.

Tip

You don't have to add a "Subject"—but it helps the recipient find your e-mail again later and reminds them what it was about. It's useful if you exchange lots of emails with someone to be able to identify which is which when all the email titles are displayed in your inbox.

Formal e-mail

Some e-mails are formal—more like business letters. The layout may be different, but the language will be the same as a letter: "Dear," "Sincerely," and so on. When you click "Send", the date and time will appear automatically along with the Subject, so you don't need to type the date into the e-mail message itself.

The e-mail address of the sender.

The e-mail address of the recipient.

Cc stands for Carbon Copy: the e-mail address(es) of others who will receive copies of the e-mail.

Bcc stands for Blind Carbon Copy: the e-mail address(es) of people who will receive a secret copy of the e-mail. (Only you and they will know they have a copy.)

From: dad@home.com

To: jack@home.com

Cc: jill@home.com

Bcc: mom@home.com

Subject: Re: surprise party

Subject is the title of your e-mail—it describes the subject matter or content in a few words. Make sure your Subject reflects the content of your e-mail. It should say what you are writing about.

Tip

E-mail to friends is generally casual. A typical greeting is "HI!"

Dear Mr. Smith,
Thank you for entertaining everyone at my party. The King Kong costume was really scary. Mom is making a good recovery!
Yours truly,
Jenna Jones
50 Willows Way, Langton, MI 10990

If you include your address, type it underneath your signature (typed at the end of the e-mail).

Springboard

Imagine two of your favorite characters from books or TV were e-mailing each other. Write an e-mail "conversation"—a series of e-mails exchanged between them.

PARTY INVITATIONS

An invitation to a special occasion is one of the nicest letters to receive! Imagining a friend's smile when they open your invitation makes them among the most satisfying letters to write, too!

Informal invitation

An invitation doesn't have to be formal. It can be quite casual.

42 Long Drive
Bloxtown, NM 73245

August 16, 2007

Dear Phoebe,

I'm having a dress-up party with a cartoon characters theme. I would love for you to come. Are you free on Saturday, September 22nd? The party is at 5 o'clock at the Town Hall. Let me know if you're able to come. Hope you're well. See you soon!

Love,

Jenny

PS I'm thinking of dressing as Snow White. If you're stuck for costume ideas give me a call!

ACTIVITY

Try designing an invitation on your computer.

- Design a letterhead using clip art or your own designs. Or cut and paste a photograph of yourself or your house at the top of the invitation.
- Add a border that fits the theme of the party.
- Print out cards with a border, but write the **text** by hand to make your invites look more personal.

Tip

If you are using a computer, you can easily print lots of copies of your invitation. Just change the name of the person you're sending it to each time.

Formal invitations are often written in the third person—

"Miss Jennifer Smith requests the pleasure of your company"

rather than the first person—

"Dear Phoebe,
I'm planning..."

Write the invitation that Cinderella never received from the Prince inviting her to the Ball. Design a letterhead fit for a prince and write the invitation on it.

☆ ★ ✩ ☆ ✩ ★ ☆

Miss Phoebe Phinn

Formal invitation

If you're planning a really glamorous party, this is the time to send out formal invitations printed on special cards.

Miss Jennifer Smith
requests the pleasure of your company
at a dress-up party
on Saturday, September 22nd
at the Town Hall

RSVP
42 Long Drive
Bloxtown, NM 73245

5:00 pm
Dress "Cartoon Characters"

RSVP

These letters stand for Répondez s'il vous plaît (French for "please reply"). The invitation may include a date by which the host or hostess would like to hear from you. For example:

RSVP August 20th

☆ ★ ✩ ☆ ✩ ★ ☆

Replying

When you reply to a formal invitation, reply in the same style. If the invitation was written in the third person, you should reply in the third person.

Phoebe Phinn thanks Jennifer Smith for her kind invitation and is pleased to accept.

August 20th

Write the date on a line of its own at the end of your reply.

FANTASY LETTERS

You have learned a lot about writing letters. How about writing some in a fantasy situation? You can **role-play**, writing in the **persona** of a fantasy character or a character who, in real life, could not write the letter themselves.

Here are some suggestions:

• Write a letter from one fantasy character to another

It could be a mermaid writing to Santa Claus, explaining about the absence of a chimney or Santa Claus writing to the mermaid to apologize for the socks he gave her last year (not much use if you have a tail!).

• Write the letter you wrote and never sent

Perhaps you wanted to vent to someone about something, but in the end, you decided it would hurt their feelings too much to send it to them. Or maybe you were writing to decline the invitation to be bridesmaid or usher at your aunt's wedding, but decided you could cope with wearing a silly dress or shirt for a few hours, after all. Have fun writing the letter...but don't send it!

• Write a letter from a pet to its owner

Maybe the pet is complaining about its living conditions or its lifestyle. For example, you could pretend to be a hamster who complains that his wheel squeaks and he needs his cage cleaned more often, a guinea pig who complains about her diet (her carrots are soft and she would like celery for a change), or a dog who requests some new places to walk—he's bored with the old ones.

• Write the letter you were never meant to see

You have found a letter which no one intended you to read. Why? Perhaps it holds some dark secret about your ancestors—were they royalty? Or is it some other family secret? Or is it a love-letter to your mother from your father long before you were born?

ACTIVITY

When you have finished, try writing some letters of reply.

If you enjoy writing stories as well as letters, you could combine the two. Try telling a story through an exchange of letters between two characters. Any other characters in the story will only be made known to the reader through what the two correspondents say about them.

Ask an adult to help you to melt candlewax to make a seal for the envelope.

Dearest Ma,

I be writing this note by candlelight as since I surprised that latest coach on the high road, not a mile from your cottage, I dare not show my face by day. It's not for nowt that they call your son The Second Dick Turpin!

Should anything happen to me afore we meet, your future is secure. The Third Oak holds some rewards three foot West of its trunk. Let it not be said that I let my dear Ma go hungry.

Do not expect me by day, but if a masked man taps upon your window in the small hours, I beg you grant him access. It will be I, your own loving son,

Tom

You could try writing the letter in ink with a pen made from a feather.

To make the paper look old, add tea stains. Ask an adult to brown your letter in a hot oven for a few minutes.

WRITING IN CODE

Ever since people learned to read and write, letters that needed to be kept secret have been written in code. Some codes are easier to crack than others. Here are some examples:

ACTIVITY

Try using one of these codes or make up a new one with a friend. To invent a letter code, write out the alphabet across or down a piece of paper. Then write your code letters or numbers beside each original letter. Now you can send each other messages to decode.

Codes that involve rearranging the layout of letters:

Earj ohni hopey oua rew elln. Extw eeki amh avingap artyw. Illy oub ea blet oc omed?

Dear John, I hope you are well. Next week I am having a party. Will you be able to come?

Dea rjo hnI hop eyo uar ewe llN ext wee kia mha vin gap art yWi lly oub eab let oco me?

Dear John, I hope you are well. Next week I am having a party. Will you be able to come?

In each sentence, the first letter of each word hops onto the end of the word before.

Raed nhoj I epoh uoy era llew. Txen keew I ma gnivah a ytrap. Lliw uoy eb elba ot emoc?

Dear John, I hope you are well. Next week I am having a party. Will you be able to come?

Every word has three letters—but it is saying the same message as before. A capital letter shows when each new sentence starts.

Again, this is the same message, but each word is spelled backwards.

Codes that involve reading some words and not others—every third word, for example:

Bananas are dear today so Leah and I please will not meet up soon. Joe is not at home for the week. Oh well!

Dear Leah, please meet Joe at the well.

A code that substitutes the next letter in the alphabet to represent each letter of the original message:

- EFBS MFBI QMFBTF NFFU KPF BU UIF XFMM

Dear Leah, please meet Joe at the well.

Tip

If you use numbers for your code, don't use them in order A=1, B=2, and so on. That's too easy to crack.

Tip

Single-letter words speed up cracking a code, so add "I" and "a" to other words to make your code harder to crack.

Coded messages that can be read in the mirror:

Dear Leah, Please meet Joe at the well.

Dear Leah, please meet Joe at the well.

Springboard

Create a **pseudonym** to conceal your identity. See if you can think of one that gives clues as to who you really are, such as an anagram of your name. For example, ALICE WARNER could be RARE LAWN ICE.

HINT: To form an anagram, write the letters of your name on separate slips of paper. Jumble them up and see what new name you can create.

Or you could try combining your pet's name with a pop star's name, such as FIDO DIDO.

SUMMING UP

Here are some final points to think about when writing a letter.

1. Picture the person you are writing to as you write.

2. In a friendly letter, write as you would speak. Don't try to use sophisticated language just because it is written down.

3. Draft your letter first on scrap paper. Then you can concentrate fully on neat, legible handwriting for the **final copy**.

4. Fold your letter so that it fits in an envelope. Practice with a spare piece first.

5. Put the date on your letter, including the year.

6. Keep your sentences short and read your letter aloud.

7. Remember, if you are writing a business letter, use a formal greeting and closing.

8. Keep business letters to one page in length.

9. Avoid starting every sentence with "I."

10. Stop and think twice before pressing "Send" on an e-mail.

Here are some further suggestions for practicing your letter-writing skills. Write a letter to:

- a child of the future—perhaps your great-great-grandchild who is not born yet

- the grandfather or grandmother who you never met

- a famous historical figure, such as Abraham Lincoln or Florence Nightingale

- your favorite fictional character

- your future self. Seal and address the envelope and write at the top: NOT TO BE OPENED UNTIL YOUR 21ST BIRTHDAY

Imagine you have just moved. You are missing your old home and friends. Write an e-mail to your best friend. You want to sound upbeat and positive. Tell him or her all about your new home and town. At the same time, let your friend know you think about him or her often. Try to strike a happy balance as you draft your e-mail.

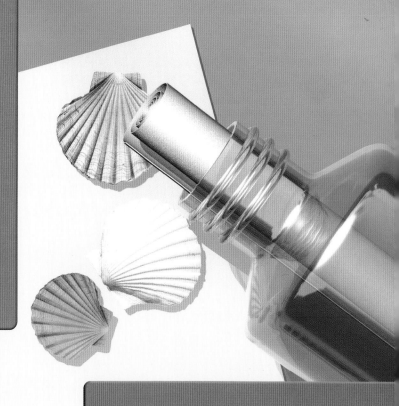

Imagine you are stranded on a desert island. All you have is writing materials. A bottle floats ashore. You write a letter, seal it in the bottle, and throw it out to sea in the hope that someone will find and read it. What will you say in your "Dear Anybody" letter?

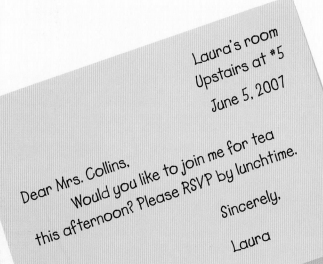

Laura's room
Upstairs at #5
June 5, 2007

Dear Mrs. Collins,
Would you like to join me for tea this afternoon? Please RSVP by lunchtime.

Sincerely,

Laura

Springboard 3

Write a letter to a member of your family in a formal style, as if you don't know them well. For example:

- A thank-you letter to Dad for cooking dinner (beginning Dear Mr.).
- A letter to your brother or sister requesting a tour of their room (beginning Dear Mr. / Miss).
- An invitation to Mom to join you for tea.

GLOSSARY

Autobiography a book written about the author's own life

BCC blind carbon copy—a secret copy of a letter or an e-mail sent to another person

CC carbon copy—an identical copy of a letter or an e-mail sent to another person

Closing the ending phrase of a letter

Comma a punctuation mark, used to show a pause

Correspond to exchange letters or e-mail

Correspondent a person with whom you exchange letters or e-mail

Draft a first, rough version of a letter, to be checked and improved

E-mail short for electronic mail

Final copy correct copy of a letter that is ready to be sent

Formal following conventional rules and using correct language

Format style, such as the layout of a letter

Greeting the opening phrase of a letter

Informal relaxed and casual style

Letterhead stationery with the address printed at the top

Opinion a personal point of view, rather than a fact

Paragraph a group of related sentences in a piece of writing

Persona character or identity

pp per persona—meaning "on behalf of." Used when a letter is signed on behalf of someone else

PS post script—meaning "after writing." Text following the main writing and after the signature. Useful for afterthoughts.

Pseudonym a false name or "pen name" used by a writer

Recipient a person who receives something

Response a reply

Role-play behaving as if you were another person

RSVP répondez s'il vous plait—meaning "please reply"

Signature someone's name, handwritten

Statement an account of facts, rather than opinions

Subject the topic about which you are writing

Tone your style of writing, which could be informal or formal

Text written words

Title a person's personal or career status, such as Mr., Mrs., Miss, Ms., Doctor, Professor, or Reverend

INDEX

PARENT AND TEACHER NOTES

- There's a reason that people talk about letter-writing as an "art"—one that is practiced less and less in these days of e-mail and text messaging. All of these forms of correspondence are part of the same basic human need to communicate with others. Correspondence, whether formal or informal, instant or considered, is explored broadly in this book. Every page informs and teaches, while encouraging children to put pen to paper or fingers to keyboard.

- Some children will be familiar with terms, such as "PS" and "RSVP," but may not know their meaning. The glossary on page 30 includes abbreviations of terms that are useful in letter-writing.

- There is much scope for creative writing in pretend letters. The more your child gets pleasure from writing letters for fun, the easier it becomes for him or her to write letters "for real."

- Encourage your child to show an interest in letter-writing that stretches beyond writing pretend letters. It would be beneficial if your child could go one step further by sending real letters to real people. Then the child can experience the pleasure of receiving a reply.

- Your child could write, for example, to a company requesting information or a catalog. This will show your child how writing a letter can bring a result. They might write to a children's magazine—and possibly see their letter in print.

- Help your child to improve their letter-writing. Knowing how to draft and edit letters, especially business ones, will help your child throughout life.

- You can help your child by providing nice paper and envelopes. Attractive stationery will help to make the writing of letters a pleasure.

- Help younger children check that the envelope is the right way up before they write the address. Provide stamps for them to mail real letters. Write back to them if they write to you.

- Perhaps you could provide your child with an address book. Help add names and addresses to encourage your child to write letters to friends and family.